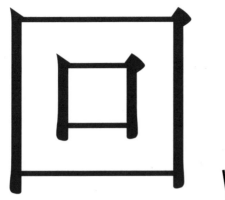

Return
Emily Lee Luan

Nightboat Books
New York

ISBN 978-1-64362-174-6

Cover design by Claire Zhang and Rissa Hochberger
Design and typesetting by Claire Zhang and Rissa Hochberger
Calligraphy by Ling-Ju Luan

Typeset in Jjannon

Cataloging-in-publication data is available from the Library of
Congress

Nightboat Books
New York
www.nightboat.org

Contents

Elision

My mother's mother grew up under Japanese occupation.

When she would open her bento box each day in school, she was met with a square of white rice and the startling smashed pink of a pickled plum in its center—to resemble her colonizer's flag.

When I ask my mother about Taiwan, her life, she waves the question away, saying, *We were just so poor, so poor.*

When I open my gaze to the past, I see with one eye, as if a hole gone through my skull.

At its end there is salt and tart to no end.

月亮 above the river the year I thought I wanted to die.

月亮 that moves my memory of my father's retelling of his father's retelling.

月亮 that appears crisp and hallowed, which I turn my gaze from for fear.

月亮 I forget about.

月亮代表我的心。

月亮 of my childhood, recited in 李白's poem.

月亮 the white of a killing frost.

月亮 the drunken poet drowned reaching for, the convenient myth.

月亮 itself only repetition with the novelty of phases.

月亮 burning opaquely in the circle of the well.

月亮 the shape my grandfather's father jumped into.

月亮 itself as sorrow, though it did not ponder to be sorrow.

月亮月亮月亮 I felt for through a sheet of black hair.

月亮 the only light that water drinks.

When My Sorrow Was Born

After Kahlil Gibran

When my Sorrow was born, I held it, a dark pearl spit from its shell, and I remembered the salt that had rounded it, centuries ago, before I even had a mouth.

And my Sorrow was unafraid and it gave me back my bravery and my anger, walked me to the tossing water and proclaimed the water mine.

My Sorrow held me and did not tell me not to cry, and the girls about me watched our sweet days together with longing, for they too wanted to be held by something with fingers as slender and delicate as my Sorrow's, fingers that tapped their temples and had them see how they had been wronged.

And those who longed for my Sorrow would never have a Sorrow like mine. I knew that, for my Sorrow had a forest-black mane like mine.

And my Sorrow let me say I, I, mine.

And my Sorrow sat with me on the fire escape all that breathing winter, and my Sorrow would not let me into the water.

And my Sorrow deveined shrimp and patterned them on my plate, brought me a wide bowl brimming with broth.

And we ate fried eggs with chopsticks. We waited for my Joy to come.

From what are you separated?

My chiropractor tells me, *Your sternum is shining,* meaning
that the small bones in my chest are rotating, overlapping,
and moving away from one another—a snared zipper.
He places the pads of his fingers beneath my collarbone, willing them.

I should love the revolution, but the revolution killed my grandfather's father.
He was just a rich man who smoked opium, read the stars, and arranged
marriages, they say, who was brought to his knees by his own village.

His sister was paraded through town with a wooden sign
around her neck. She knelt in the center for hours.
The sign was hung by a metal wire; it slowly sank
until her skin parted and bared the bone in the back of her neck.

Oh, I love you, *Ling Ling,* the man on the street says to me.

I've said it before: I don't know where I am.

The moon landing of me;
the walls long and clean.
Again, the quiet night
ruined by my anger.

-

A tongue feeling—numbness dressed in waves.

-

Most days I forget the kitchen table. I cried there,
almost nightly, for years. In the decades since my father
came to this country, the only English book
he ever bought was a self-help volume on raising
problem children. I remember the blond toddler
on the cover—her face twisted, mouth at the edge
of opening into a scream.

-

In the schoolyard, the kids chanted

  fight fight fight

and I kicked and kicked
him until his face turned
young and sad.

-

My mother had my ears pierced at age nine to cure me of my temper.
Now the old ache greens in my chest.
I have been cutting my hair to be kinder.

-

milk carton mouth
paper and wide open

-

At the temple, grey-haired women shook demons from the air around
me—their blue smocks, surgical masks.

-

My mother: a riot
at the grocery store cash register. Yes, I watched
from behind the turning conveyor belt,
her broken English. But is there a word
for an anger rooted in sadness? Is there forgiveness
for us in either of our languages?

-

I broke his knee then because he named me what I am.
And his hand at my throat: a plea, if not
an apology for what I am.

-

9

Late night, in the rain, I walk as a child does, forgetting to watch my step, looking instead at the glare on the inside of my glasses, trying to understand its green blur of light. My recklessness—a curiosity toward small destruction.

-

That feeling when the sink begins to drain—I love it.

Reversible Poem in Dishwater

He carried me into the kitchen to get a glass of water
He reached for a cup in the sink filled with dishwater
Wait I said and opened the cabinet for a glass
Still he went for the cup in the sink
Why do you want to drink from a dirty glass I asked
It doesn't need to be clean he said
But accepted the clean one I held out to him

I held out a clean glass to him
He accepted he said clean is a need isn't it
I asked to drink from a dirty glass
I want you
The sink the cup still a glass cabinet open
I waited filled with dishwater
The cup sinking he reached for me
The kitchen carried me into the glass

Google Search: My Sadness

my sadness
my sadness comes in waves
        was never beautiful
        is overwhelming
        quotes
        turns into anger
        is a suitcase
        knows no bounds
        has become an addiction

Young Asian American Women: Under Double Pressure ...
A Hidden Tragedy—Mental Illness and Suicide Among ...
[PDF] Asian American Women and Depression FACT SHEET - ...
Asian American Teenage Girls Have Highest Rates ... - NAMI
Top 10 Myths about Asian Americans and Mental Health
Why Are Asian-American Women Prone to Suicidal ...
I Thought Being Miserable Was Just Part Of Being Chinese ...

Google Search: My Sadness is

my sadness is luminous
        is like
        is
        is your happiness
my pain and sadness is more

Myth: Young Asian-American women (aged 15-24) have the highest suicide rates of all racial/ethnic groups (American Psychological Association).

My Sadness is _____

I think about being sad, all the time. Sometimes I'm afraid I'm not actually sad but that I'm sad because I tell myself: I am sad. My sadness is the radiator in my room that spouts water and knocks loudly on its own insides. It's the phantom leak above my desk, the water damage it left in my books.

I can't find the crack in the ceiling.

I'm worried my mother knows I worry about her.

FACT SHEET- ...

My sadness is my refrigerator
                is a sink!
                is
                is cold hands
                turns into anger
                is a pinecone
                is a pear
                is a square
                is ugly
                doesn't fit
                doesn't fit
                doesn't fit

ugly ugly ugly ugly
ugly ugly ugly ugly
ugly ugly ugly ugly
ugly ugly ugly ugly

窟

Sometimes a hole sounds like cry,
a long string of o's stacked
high as an echo, with a dirt end
to the puckered lip not nearly in sigh.

Sometimes a hole sounds like cry,
the throat the hard k that round
walls bloom from.

Sometimes a hole sounds like cry—
what cradles water, what tunnels water.

Sometimes a hole sounds like cry
in this order: where the needle enters;
one who speaks for the to-be buried;
two rising mountains.

Sometimes a hole sounds like cry,
enamored with the narrow
of its voice.

Sometimes a hole sounds like cry,
like a long postal road.

Sometimes a hole sounds like cry,
dry, dry.

A ring softens to the contours of my finger. A true gold is a soft metal. Nothing fully unyielding. Even my mother, who knew I lied, often believed me. But no character looks a perfect O. I'd close my big □ with 3 clean strokes.

My body—a flight attendant's body,

one of the ones on a Chinese airline.

I watched them last time I was on an international

flight—their skinny arms and flat chests, their clean

sense of purpose. I had an aisle seat

and they bumped my elbow

with the beverage cart, said sorry to me in two

languages, both of them mine.

I thought, *I could be a flight attendant,*

and in another life, I might've been.

My cousin is a flight attendant on Eva Air.

My other cousin, born three days before me

who wants to be a model, tried to be a flight attendant

instead. But she didn't get it, said there was too much

memorization and she couldn't remember everything.

I secretly know I'd be a great flight attendant.

I could discreetly close the overhead

bins, twist my hair back, tie the service

apron on, hand out hot towels, blink

my eyes big, say *tea tea* 茶茶

all the way down the aisle.

When offering small sandwiches

I might stare out of one of the windows,

imagine the ocean blue. Or, say, when cleaning

up a toddler's vomit, I might yearn

for a less solitary life. But otherwise, loneliness

might be okay when surrounded by other

flight attendants in the sky, my body

a body made for tending to bodies in flight.

I'd breathe in the air of neither

here nor there. I'd remember everything

about my lives on earth.

SOUTH CHINA SEA SOUTH CHINA SEA SOUTH CHINA SEA SOUTH CHINA SEA SOUTH CHIN
A SEA SOUTH CHINA SEA SOUTH CHINA SEA SOUTH CHINA SEA SOUTH CHINA SEA SOUTH
CHINA SEA SOUTH CHINA SEA SOUTH CHINA SEA SOUTH CHINA SEA SOUTH A SOUTH CHINA
SEA SOUTH CHINA SEA SOUTH CHINA SEA SOUTH CHINA SEA SOUTH CHINA SEA SOUTH
SOUTH CHINA SEA SOUTH CHI... CHINA SEA SOUTH CHI...
SOUTH CHINA SEA SOUTH CHINA SEA SOUTH CHINA SEA SOUTH CHINA SEA SOUTH CHIN
A SEA SOUTH CHINA SEA SOUTH CHINA SEA SOUTH CHINA SEA SOUTH CHINA SEA SOUTH CHIN
CHINA SEA SOUTH CHINA SEA SOUTH CHINA SEA SOUTH CHINA SEA SOUTH A SOUTH CHINA OUTH
SEA SOUTH CHINA SEA SOUTH CHINA SEA SOUTH CHINA SEA SOUTH CHINA SEA SOUTH SOUT
OUTH C

A long dirt road lined with thin trees, blurred figure on a bike.

現 在 家 鄉 的 道 路

[now]   [now]   [no-]   [now]   [now]   [now]   [w]

21

五十年後　　　　我與　　　　二妹　　　三妹　　　合影
　years later　　　　　　　2nd sister　3rd sister　　take a group photo

Torn red paper on a wooden door

THE ONLY OLD HOUSE THAT'S LEFT OF MY HOME.

家中僅存下的老屋

A child

in yellow
in the courtyard

23

[everybody!—   navy blue]

家   族   合   影   FAMILY   GROUP   PHOTO
     FAMILY   合   影   家   族   GROUP
PHOTO   家   家   家   家   家   家

My grandfather in a suit and tie when he returned home

捨得

In her fifty-ninth year, my mother loves the idea of letting go. She likes saying things like

錢可以解決的問題，不是問題。

你捨得，還是捨不得？

But she calls me, tells me she can't believe my aunt threw the dirty dish towels in the wash with her laundry.

She wishes my father still held her hand.

She says, *Don't tell your sister about my silly problems. I don't want her to worry.*

She carves two stone seals:

one with our family name and the branches of the tree
we're named after; the other with the two characters 捨得。

So she won't forget.

Can you bear parting with it? Or can you not?

捨不得 to throw the tomato in the trash when it's gone soft.
捨不得 to wear my white shoes when it's raining.
捨不得 to leave the sidewalk where the heavy sunflower blooms in August.

27

捨不得
捨不得

Her younger brother was an alcoholic. All the sisters pooled money so
that he could go to rehab, but he still drank himself to death. They found
him on the side of the road, his skin yellowed.

I know she was once willing to part with the silk shirts she brought here
from Taiwan—their patterned sleeves and shifting seams.

She's the only one who hears me sing.
The only one who hears me singing, she.

Only one, who hears my song?
One hears me sing—no, she's the only.

Who, me? I'm my only.
Hear me sing her only song.

I sing, and there's my only, hearing.
Sing her to only.

Sing me into hearing
I who is my only.

Hearing why my onlys, she sings.
Whose hearing ones to singing?

One, the only one,
Only my only sing me.

The she who sings, hearing all the way to one.
She's singing, in it I hear my onely.

I can't remember if he pulled
my hair and on which night—
I'm like that these days.

He might know what parts
of me to touch. When to turn me
over. Or not. All I ever remember

is that it's blue, and then it's
morning. The long train ride home.
I never imagined this would be

what I was promised in high school
locker rooms—the unparticular dark,
the seeping, the sinking knees.

In those days, I knew it was shameful
for a boy to call me pretty, because
then he'd like girls like me, with

different parents. I felt ashamed, too,
for the ones who didn't understand
that desiring me was dangerous,

if I saw them staring at the bloomers
under my uniform as I snapped in
and out of the sky, in and out of the arms

of girls more lovable than me.
The only rule of cheerleading
was to never let me hit the ground.

But that wasn't the kind of
untouchable I wanted to be. I wanted
to be pressed against. Jarred. An object

thrown without fear of glass
breaking. At practice, Michelle did splits
on the blue spring floor as she told me

about her first time. *It hurts,*
she said. And I wanted it because
she had it. Anyway, could it hurt more

than I already did, shaking
my maroon-and-silver pom-poms
as if the shimmer could transform me

into an earthly animal? Every time
they put me up, I wanted to come
down, painted across the field

in the flood of stadium lights,
the vacant blue of desire spreading
as wide as a country.

I watched the ceiling from my low bed. It bent when the girls danced upstairs.

I looked out that window for a year, saw the water low under the bridge.

I stayed as still as I could under the bedspread.

The shower below the stairwell, as if a foot could, through the ceiling.

I washed the dishes in the round basin sink and found it beautiful, an inverted bridge.

Bent myself into a dance, watched the water.

My plywood desk splintered and sagged.

Threw up blueberries on the tile one day; I worried the heater would light the curtains on fire.

I guess it was spring then, but who can ever tell unless the river is rising?

I heard laughter, out of my mouth.

The light was so bright in the mornings that the tulips opened into small, petaled basins.

Yes, I watched the moon, stilling to its height.

My face round after the night, and I tried the trick with spoons, as if cold water could.

Because

I had no appetite, my
stomach shrunk to the size
of a bird's. Because I hated
eating eggs, I'd been a chicken
in my past life. The ghouls
would come if I whistled
at night. Born in the year
of the monkey, my butt
must've been as red
as a baboon's. A palm
smoothing my back
could steal the anger away;
otherwise, I didn't like
to be touched. My father
said he'd put hot sauce
on my thumb if I kept
sucking it. If that didn't work,
he'd cut it off. I loved lambs
and worms. A boy called me
Asian so I broke his knee.
I thought myself a chicken,
clucking for the eggs
separated from me.

Target™ Haibun

I like driving around, especially in my yoga pants. I like getting out of the car, locking it, dangling my keys from my middle finger, walking through the parking lot and into Target. When I'm longing, I like the bright lights and linoleum floors, the way the red doors whoosh open for me. Inside, I touch the lipsticks, uncapping and turning them, putting the hues to the back of my hand. I buy two tension rods to hang long curtains from. I ask, *Are these the only options I have in store?* It's easy to buy the wrong thing, as easy as feeling eighteen again, driving to buy cigars in my dad's old Camry. When I'm longing, I'm in that car again, waiting to bloom in the chest, crying about a bright-haired boy until my body is hot. If I just had American parents, I could be loved. Maybe. *Are these the only options I have in store?* Somehow, after all this time, I still believe in an objective kind of beauty. In the makeup aisle, I see a woman with yellow hair and astonishing eyes. How cruel that she wears those colors, and with such ease.

I hang my curtains
One to black out the morning
I hang them—grey, white

I Put Tasks I Do for Free into a Folder Titled "Jobs"

There are not enough hours in the day before I have to perform affection.

That's an objectively robotic thing to say, my therapist tells me, when I speak about my responses to sentimentality.

My weekly battle with the laser printer—a kind of intimacy, my pleading.

I don't want your flashing red light, I say, *telling me you won't go.*

I wear shoes I found on a sidewalk. That must mean something, my feet bathed in the ghost of someone else's feet.

When Cynthia, the taller and much-older cousin, looked under the deck and saw that the baby birds in the nest had their heads bitten off, I screamed until someone inevitably told me to stop.

I've always been this sensitive, hands clapped over my ears.

A pure emotion, like thread trickling from a spider, is rare and terrifying in its precision.

After the particularly stressful movie, I provoked a fight.

Or, should I say, the fight lived in me, and then it was rattled out of me by the screen performance of other griefs.

All emotion feels to me a kind of performance. I'm trying to unlearn that now.

At the cafe, my laptop screen kisses the screen of the laptop across from mine. *Mwah.* Though the other screen already has its partner.

The acupuncturist smoothing tiger balm on my shoulders every week. That could be enough to live for.

Who will love me when my Wi-Fi code runs out?

I break my grandmother's $100 bill on squash and eggs. She touched that bill; I saved it as a greedy child; that money goes quickly from me now, as she went from me, as she's now gone.

I thought: that money is little to me now, and the thought rattled out a nest of bitten-off sadness.

I was in Chinatown when the building with the archives burned, but I didn't see the smoke. *That's where those beautiful archives are,* I'd said to my companion, and pointed freely.

Who am I to declare against your need
of me, mined. You and I, a likely objective.
It's easy to meet that in-between, where
the something-like-being lies. You gun
the coffee, I music the day, the heavy cloud
warbles in my chest, grows fingers for you.
What is it other than a misunderstanding—
all love, we madden towards it, outside
our webbed instincts. I wouldn't say
I know, but then again, a blue light braves
the light line; someone calls to say
call facilities. Which is to say,
the latch is fixable, time is fixed,
a long list we cross to be missed.

浪漫

romance is slow water
water the under ask
ask me do I have belief
belief a feathery root
rooting around a vastness
vastly said another night held
held to a foldable line
lining the silver bank
bank not light light not fast
fasting my feeling
feeling a drawn form
formless the tide overfull
over-spooled by a lover
lover a non-belief

Ruthless

My friend lowers his foot into the stony
runoff from the mountain, lets out a burst
of frantic laughter. This, I think, is a happiness.

When I don't feel pain, is it joy that pours
in? A hollow vessel glows to be filled.
無， my father taught me, is tangible—

an emptiness held. It means *nothing,* or *to not have*,
which implies there was something to be had
in the first place. It negates other characters:

無心， "without heart";
無情， "without feeling";
heartless, ruthless, pitiless.

Is the vacant heart so ruthless?

The ancient pictogram for 無 shows a person
with something dangling in each hand. Nothingness
the image of yourself with what you once had,

what you could have. And the figure is dancing,
as if to say nothingness is a feeling, maybe even
a happiness—dancing with what is gone from you.

When I ask myself, *What am I missing?* I think
of how much I loved to dance, arms awash
with air, the outline of loss leaping on the wall.

39

I spend the night following leaks in the ceiling. I put
a tin can under the drip but it's too loud and keeps me
up. The night pours itself on the window screen
and the trees wave, un-astounded. I read: weeping
is a non-coincidence with the feeling of the nearness
of terror. I haven't wept in months.

Another night a rabbit screams a near-human scream.
The thought of a coyote hearing the sound and yet still
clawing at its beating neck—it keeps me up. The next
morning I don't want to find the severed animal
in the grass so I step gingerly, eyes to the tree line.

I twist my wrist twisting a branch off a tree—
coincidence? The leaves drip on me in great big splashes,
wetting the back of my neck. Near the tree, I can barely hear
its beating. I lean in, pour myself onto its great cracked feet.

哭

The line was always 不要哭。 It made me 哭。

2 mouths + 1 dog = 哭

2 mouths = 2 eyes

1 big mark = 1 dog

The first time I 哭 it's remarkable to you.

You say I've never seen you 哭。

And then I never stop 哭 I am safe to 哭 my face barks and barks and barks.

So sick of my 哭 you say OK 不要哭。

不要。不要。不要。

I 哭 and 哭 and 哭。

It did not turn. It raced red and red and red. For many months, my limbs were full and hot and I heard the world as if through the belligerence of water. I became the same child I once was, with an anger so bright it once made my father put his fist through a wall. There, that was the power—that a scream could make a man remember his hands, that it could sleep in my body for one decade and then another, that, after all that time, it could still cleave my sternum in two. I became luminous, a cold light on cedar. And wasn't that what I'd always wanted, to glow with a terrifying light, to startle even the freckled girls of my childhood, for whom all the happiest objects seemed reserved? I knew that telling sadness it was beautiful made it dangerous. But I needed it. I pet it; all along, it was a long black horse. I combed its pitched mane, fed it carrots, let it pull sugar from my palm so it could run and run

Types of Return

回口回口回口回口回口
回春回春回春回春回春
回首回首回首回首回首
回去回去回去回去回去

回國回國回國回國回國
回歸回歸回歸回歸回歸
回落回落回落回落回落
回音回音回音回音回音

回答回答回答回答回答
回復回復回復回復回復
回家回家回家回家回家
回路回路回路回路回路

回來回來回來回來回來
回來回來回來回來回來

迴文

Let me tell you about the river.
How it returns, brutally.
There was a time my friends
skinny-dipped in the river.
I was jealous not to have
been there. At the time, it burned
to be seen naked, my darker
nipples. How it returns, brutally,
the low image of my body
in those months. I never curled
onto the fire escape above
the river, though I imagined
it often, and it is now memory.
There was a time I climbed down
the back of the bridge and waded
in the underbelly of the river's
waterfall, which marks a hysterical
happiness. The river—I once
sampled its water for oxygen.
Let me tell you about the shrill
clarity of sadness. And how it is
reduced to a singular image.
Let me tell you about the river
in January. Let me tell you of
its color at night. When the spring
came I watched the water swell high.
This image—it made me sick.

何處別魂銷？

I bring my grandfather to a restaurant on 8th. It's a hole-in-the-wall kind of joint—a pizza place with candlelight. I can't eat anything here, I tell him as we walk through the wall and into the hole, I'm gluten and lactose intolerant now. You can't eat even 山東's famous beef noodle soup? he asks. No, not even, I say. That's okay, I can't eat either, I'm dead! he replies, and ducks into the bricked darkness.

何處別魂銷？

My grandfather brings me to the old family well. It's just a cylinder of stones in a yellow field, and the sky is grey. We are in no country. My mother used to carry water from this well, he says. We stand around it, but we don't peer in, and there is a silence—like watching the ocean fold from behind glass—between us. Sometimes it feels like different phases of the same sadness, I finally say, and we draw crescents around the rim of the well with our eyes.

何處別魂銷？

My grandfather and I eat a steamed trout. We start with the meat on one side of the bone. When we finish, we flip the fish together, my chopsticks on the tail, his wedged in the hollow beneath its jaw. As we eat, moving towards the head, our language unhinges—his accent grows northern, bright on the second syllable; mine dissolves, mouth gone to water. By the time I empty the tender meat of the cheek, my grandfather is tapping rhythms for me with his chopsticks against the spine of the fish. I offer him a fish eye. Together, we chew them to seed. Each of our eyes, in their dead way, swivels and blinks to each other from our stomachs.

何處別魂銷？

My grandfather and I eat fried pork and rice at the train station. The rice, short-grain and chewy, was grown in the fields surrounding the station. After, we climb the wooden viewing pagoda and stare out at the current of meticulous green shoots—rows and rows to the horizon. The water flooding the fields mirrors the pitch of grey clouds above. A long hush as the wind silvers its way through the leaves. One of us thinks—what an arresting scene—and the other agrees.

A man arrives in a small truck. We watch as he steps into a white suit that zips over his face, with a window to look out of. He mixes something blue in a bucket, pours it into a metal cannister, straps it to his back, and climbs into the green, roving up and down the aisles of rice shoots to spray the field with color. The wind picks up. We shield our noses from the chemical smell.

Back in town, the stray dogs stand up and stare as we walk past.

何處別魂銷？

I stand with my grandfather on 五指 mountain. He holds up his outstretched hand. 五指, he says, five fingers, so that I can understand. We look beyond the clouds shrouding the mountain, past 徐奶奶's stone grave. Are you okay with being here forever? I ask. I'm not sure I have a choice, he replies, and grasps all ten of his fingers together.

51

銷魂別處何？

My grandfather and I board the train down the coast. We have our 飯糰, our soy milk. I sit beside a boy my age and we both read books. I imagine we're young lovers in a Taiwanese film, drawing open the curtain and looking out together when the ocean comes.

I can see the top of my grandfather's baseball cap a few rows ahead of me. Sometimes he disappears, slouching down to sip his soy milk.

We enter dark tunnels in the crowded mountains, and until I see the white sky, I fear we will never surface.

When I walk down the aisle to his row, my grandfather is gone. A wad of plastic wrap and an empty milk box.

From the train, the ocean, and as we ride, the farther from it.

I Narrate the Memory of My Grandparents' Neighbor's Birds Again

All I can see now is the plastic roof
that bathes their neighbor's sitting room
in blue-green light; it traps the heat
where the cockatiels sing. Let's say this

is the country—my grandparents,
their neighbors, my parents, my sister,
and I sit inside the heat that lives
inside the summer of a country. We eat

rice noodles. We unravel the stained skin
of dragon fruit to our feet. We spit
chicken bones into boxes folded
from the pages of magazines. My grandfather

tells my father a story about the war,
and my father turns to tell my sister
and me. 徐奶奶 feeds the cockatiels
each morning so they'll keep on singing.

At night, when they sleep, we close
our eyes and cover our faces with
our arms. On long and humid days,
we grow tired of telling stories, grow

tired of the singing. The days stack
on top of one another like stones
in a well. The blue-green light turns sour
so our faces glow like we're in a city,

eating snacks outside a corner store.
We wonder when we'll go to our homes
to leave 徐奶奶 to feed her birds
alone. We wonder what home, which

country. The birds, were they even
cockatiels? I see their plumage a golden
yellow, like the violent light that burns down
into evening over my grandparents'

concrete courtyard, the courtyard long
gone to rubble, their courtyard the border
of all memory, the birds all I can hear beside.

I curse the day on which I saw the sun,
for it makes me seem a man raised in the woods.
—Petrarch

I.

Always, the predisposition
                              toward loneliness. I know now
I'm in the world,
                    that the woods are also
of this world. It's possible
                              to be without and not know
what you're missing,
                      to live with the part
of yourself
            that trails behind.
I miss
              the humid city, the ash trees
in winter, his hair leaving
                            the smell of pool water
on my pillow.
                  From a distance,
the earth could be bathed
                          in salt
or snow.
          I am of two minds about it.

II.

Once, I spent the night
                    with a man who I knew,
so clearly, was lonely,
                    who possessed a hunger
so bright
             I looked away.
Cruelty like the color
                blue, the silhouette
of the tall cactus
                by the bed. I debated morning.
I stayed.
             In the night, my apartment buzzer
rings, and my utter
                  elation at its sound startles me, saddens
me to the walls. Empty
                    caller, the leaves of my living
room grow up to meet me.

Sunflowers

The grey night, walking home, we found
sunflowers leaning against the fence as heavy
as heads. In the morning, you held my head
in your palm, and we stared at each other down
the long length of your arm. We swayed together,
if only for a little while. Then you kissed my toe
and left. I pulled the comforters out after.
You had sweat the bed; the room bloomed
with your sweetness. I thought, *You can know
somebody for a long while and not know their scent.*
I thought, *Love, is it for me? Could anybody ruin
me?* A week later, the sunflowers were gone,
overhead, just sky. In the driveway next
to the empty stalks was the family that lived
in the blue house behind the garden. A little boy
played with a fire truck. His mother and father
smiled at me as they held the de-petaled heads—
fondly, combing their soft faces. On the ground,
so many seeds! It felt like the final revelation
for a long while. We laughed together, then,
the mother, father, and I, and the sunflowers
laughed too, because they knew the loss was not
a loss after all, and the sunflower seeds, too, joined
in, opening their pinched mouths, and all together
we were a high chorus and they sang to me
as I continued down the road, the many feet
of their voices carrying my small heartbreak.

A man in the deep end sinks to the bottom of the pool
Water breaches my inner ear
I watch him but only underwater
I'm tender underwater
No man in my bed last night
Most men want to be alone except
in the hour of morning when a face dissolves to blue
When I'm gone, I'm gone, and I can't wake up
Sometimes I have dreams
and I wake up laughing

Sometimes I can't wake up
To be gone, to ask for gone but instead
laugh into blue, dissolution
My face rubbed out
Come morning, the hour of aloneness
—exceptional want
No tenderness, no night in my ear
No water, no water
To breach the end of water
To instead be pooled, deep and under

on a beautiful Wednesday early afternoon—after a night of drinking and falling asleep during the softly-filmed movie featuring salt flats—the exam gown flowered at my waist.

This year, no peonies to cut from their stakes. I buy a dozen plain seltzer cans for $7.99 even though I meant to search for a deal.

There is a left-handed actor in the movie and I wish I wrote like her, with my left hand.

I'm explaining to my students what I think it means to be political, wonder if I believe it or if it's merely creation.

Avoid calling the insurance company and avoid calling again, my pain barely tolerated because of my investment in hiding external pain.

What would it be like to do a single thing completely, to say, *Politics has to do with power,* and really, really know what you meant when you said it.

Like how sometimes when I'm alone it is just that—alone. And I feel like water all at once and before.

And the hurt is not so hard to come by. Despite it being hard work.

What does it mean to be called sensitive, when all emotional overreactions are merely reactions to a hierarchy of events.

I'm dreaming the old boyfriend has a new girlfriend and I'm enacting fury in response to her shame. I'm pleased with how cleanly I've reassembled his shoulders, his good brown hiking coat.

I know what's coming next and know he still tends to me.

There is anger above and below me but, in the dream, I know I am dreaming.

Doing takes a different kind of pain, a pain to end all pain.

And she's saying, *Does this hurt? This should hurt.* And, *I'm so sorry,* as I crinkle the paper gown.

In trying to reassemble the last sensation, all I'm remembering is the copay—the number blooms to me at times in dreams.

I think about modeling for money, and I think about it more and know myself more, and then I know myself less.

And I'm extending my hand, and what does it mean to know which one.

苦痛　　痛苦
苦難　　艱苦
苦澀　　悲苦
苦悶　　愁苦
苦惱　　困苦
苦頭　　受苦
苦笑　　吃苦
苦命　　辛苦

A toiling	an astringent lowness
A labored	misery. My love used to
Bloom	overnight, the streets wide
Enough	for me to walk down. Life
A bloody	toe or two. Easy. But I've been
Making	my mother's bitter
Melon:	halved, hollowed out,
Sautéed	with garlic, salt, the eyes of
Fermented	black beans opening
To me	from the pan. It's not
Sugar	I crave, but an ache that
Still makes	the tongue water.
A sadness	held in the mouth. Is this
Savor my	ceaseless condition? If so, I'm
Sick	with it. Pull out my molars.
Make of	me a simpler O.

I could make my way through the grass.
Could my way through the grass be mine?

Make me thoroughly grassless.
My way through—the grass I make.

Wayless, grass through my making.
Throughout the grass—*I could I could I could.*

The grass is mine to make.
Grass, I couldn't make my way through you!

Grassless me, away.
The way through me is to make me grass.

Through my making a could, grassing
wayward, through to me.

My make is grass, all the way through.
Makeless me, the through-grass weighs me.

Could I grass, could I way-make?
I grass, I way-through, I make.

Ars Poetica

I'm so absorbed in the feeling
of things I forget to see the shading
of trees—I watch the boughs just to sense
their swaying. I've taken too much
from what moves outside my window;
I've asked a leaf to make me better. I've been
bitter, sick for home, bought flower bulbs
just to capture them folding inside out.
Someone asks me, *What does a laurel
look like?* I can't answer, say, *It must be leafy
and green.* Am I selfish? Can I say I gave
and gave? I'm so sorry. Walk me along
the barren summer to the cacti withering
on the avenue. I'll break my finger into bleeding.

What does a laurel forget? I selfish a leaf
into bleeding, absorb its shades of green.
I watch the boughs so sorry I bitter, fold
inside out. The swaying makes me sick
and leafy, a tree in summer. Do I stop
my barren finger from flowering? The avenue
bulbs into withered feeling. I've said too much
to the window.

Can the boughs fold into feeling?
A barren bulb. I'm a window, apologizing.
I'm sickened by the flower on the avenue.
It sways like a lonely finger.

Clearly all about me winter reigns
四面又明明是嚴冬

I loved my mother the most at my most sad.

Nobody looked like my mother so my mother became my sorrow.

I looked in the soup on the stove and became my mother.

That winter, I slept with the mattress on the floor, a hat on at night.

The brightest mornings, the yolk splitting a violent yellow.

At some point I realized there were many things I didn't like about myself.

I read an essay about a kite.

My hair unfurled, longer and longer.

My back turned, looming taller, scalding glass jars in the sink.

Massive in my memory, hair so dark it blued.

Whose love startles in these grey sheets?
An imprint of a body on a bed. Like memory,
the body gone, over the first step, then
the second, streaming into the beet-red
of summer. Rainwater spirals like so many
long necks, pools at street corners; birds,
like smoke, plume into the cavernous sky.
What else can house the longing of the living
but the leaves that greet rooftops in the way
a kiss meets the forehead of a daughter?
A neighbor leans out of a window, the blowing
wind reminding them of former homes. Oil
separates into its violet hues; an echo
returns in the stairwell.

How does she return, to the windowed
room, the elderly neighbor walking his daughter
up the stairs? Is it a homecoming when only
the oily leaves of the pothos spiral down
to greet her? Of course, the room seems more
cavernous without her living, her longing blowing
smoke into corners. Where she's coming from,
she found the puddle of a barely-born bird, red
as a beet, in the path to the house, ants streaming
from its tiny neck. She stepped over it the first time,
but when she came back, it was gone. Standing
above the bed, she tries to remember the imprint
of her former body on the grey sheet. *Who is
the bed?* she asks, *Does it love me?*

In	that	year	I	read	Ovid
I	wanted	to	be	denied	my
form	I	was	inside	out	In
transformation	no	reversal	But	in	terror
transformation	the	inevitable	form	Reversal	too
impossible	as	turning	to	indelible	stone

I   I   read

I   wanted   denied

transformation

transformation

form

                                     form

impossible   stone

denied

no   reversal

Reversal

70

the   form   too

                          indelible

I can't go back

72

How do I do the math to bring me back to my grandfather

My father told us stories: 西遊記, boys
born from peaches, the sticky rice thrown
into the river so the fish wouldn't eat the poet's
sinking body, a holy man who was strung
on a cross. Our favorite was always the one
with the two men who dug a hole in the ground.
They dug and dug until they found a door
and the door opened into a world where black
was white and up was down and sugar was not
sweet but bitter.

I tried to find the seam, the dark fold beneath.

It begins, 有一天

One day—

One day my grandfather's father jumps down
the family well. He stands on the wall of the well
and suddenly drops away, into the ground,
as if he has fallen into a hole that runs through
the center of the earth.

A tube of dark water, viewed from below. A small column of light and open hands, electric.

We pan out to see that the tube of water is in fact a quiet lake at night, a small moon making milk of its surface.

I watched *Tim Burton's The Nightmare Before Christmas* in Taipei with my cousin. We sat too close to the TV and sucked on sugar cane while he complained that the English was too fast for him, the Mandarin subtitles appearing in flashing blocks at the bottom of the screen. How can there be a Halloween town and a Christmas town parallel to one another, separated only by a door—can one exist a mere portal away from the other?

But I was here, wasn't I? Barefoot in December, spitting out sugarcane pulp in the Taiwanese heat.

If I dig a hole to China—

If the Chinese Civil War happened between 1927 and 1950 and your grandfather was ninety-three when he died in 2007, then in what year did he save a soldier from drowning? In what year did he flee from his native Shandong (where his father jumped down the family well) and how did he receive his island nation?

My father pours milk into the center of my bowl of grass jelly. In our big backyard, the blue lantern zaps insects to charcoal.

At night, I dream of men falling through dark tunnels.

All I have of my grandfather: watching him halve
dragon fruit in the tiled kitchen, rolling a pencil against
his big toe to knead out the knots. The malls in the south
of Taiwan and the shoes he promised to buy me; his garden
of tomatoes and flowers and the big clay pot of koi fish
in the courtyard, how he'd let me scatter their food onto
the surface of the water. When he knelt to take a photo, he'd turn
his baseball cap backward. How he struck all the dinner off
the table the time my father dared say his full name aloud.
On his deathbed, he mumbled only of his life in China, a sea away.

In 1958, Mao Zedong orders a mass extermination of sparrows. They eat small grains and seeds—dark-beaked thieves. Farmers and peasants tear down their nests and shoot them from the sky. They take to the fields with drums and pots and pans; the sky knuckles with sound. The sparrows swarm scared into the air and fly and fly and fly until their bodies drop to the ground.

I did not know how to cry for my grandfather in America. Lung cancer sounds to me like an American disease.

The last time I saw him I took a video of him moving through the courtyard with his walker, waving to me every time I called out to him. A few months later, back home, my parents threw me a party for my thirteenth birthday. They recorded me, squirming and embarrassed, as everybody sang to me in the candlelit dark. The birthday footage was recorded over that of my grandfather, and when I think of it now I still want to scream.

I accidentally said 好 to my kindergarten teacher instead of *Yes, I will.*

The poet's sinking body

My father tells me, *The night before my father left to join the KMT army, my grandmother showed him several barrels of gold, silver, and antiques and asked him to dig holes in the ground to bury the barrels. The landmark was a well and a big tree. When my father went back to his village sixty years later he couldn't find the well and the tree anymore. Think about this, we could be rich with all the gold, silver, and antiques. Ha ha.*

In the war, my grandfather saved a soldier from drowning in the lake. Another man tried to grab onto him too, but he could only save one without all three of them sinking.

My aunt carried my grandfather's
favorite flowers back from Pingtung
and planted them in her yard in Houston.
They're a streaky pomegranate red
and have tapered petals and long filaments
like a tiger lily does. *It's so strange,* she tells me,
it's the perfect temperature for them here.

One day my grandfather's father jumped down the family well. And did
my grandfather regret not saving him from his drowning.

A small column of light

I lived by a river that year and the water at night—it moved.

I try to place the years my grandfather's father slept in a barn filled with cows. At night, men would find him, pour water on his face, and clang their empty pots above him. Every night like this, sleepless and half-alive, rolled in on himself like a coiled spine. The noise a white light that tunneled through his ears.

Were there commercial airlines in Asia in 1950 or did they take ships

A hole so deep I may one day meet him in the middle.

Locus Amoenus with Migrating Deer

So much was set in winter:
My sister and I standing
in the white yard feeling

small and alive as only
children can, the snow
blaring down as we brought

carrots into the woods,
tied them up with gold
string for the migrating

deer. In the kitchen, my father
chanted a Taoist prayer;
my mother worried the floors.

I sleep alone now, as I did
in those years, each morning
peeling open like a quiet road.

At the train station, I'm always
terrified someone will jump
in front of the coming train—

more for myself than for them.
I hope no one will push me
in front of the coming train

because then I'll know
it is possible. How many years
have I slept alone? I feel safe only

in knowing that my father, too,
fears death. Far away, my mother
strings carrots across the trees.

We never went back to see
if they were gone. The deer
leave patterns in the yard.

My father used to be a manager at a beverage factory. At the end of the day when everyone else had left, he'd fill one of the vats with leftover milk and steam it until it was hot. Then he'd leave his clothes on the factory floor and take a long milk bath.

Every so often I remember this story and won't know if I've dreamt it—my father in the milk fog and silver machinery. Those were the days my father ran up debts of beer and cigarettes at the local store and before my long-haired mother began working at the factory. I imagine his body disappearing into white, his full head of black hair the first exclamation of a calligrapher's brush on rice paper. Did he long for a woman who could become my mother? Did small sounds in the silence frighten him? I want to inherit loneliness from the scene, but what do I know of my father's dreams? I'm still creating my own mythology of moving water, the field mice tunneling through ice in deep winter. When I draw a bath, I'm usually trying to take myself from sadness and into sleep. And in the blackest hour of morning my head calls back my body, like the bird that circles high above, singing 回，回，回。

Sadness, when you come back for me, I'll be among
      the cornfields, wondering about crop circles,
long toes, my mother,   and other alien things.

                It will be July, the dusk boundless and moving
           into a horizon so transparent its edge will frighten
                you. I admit: I'll be naked, swallowed

by mosquitoes, a constellation growing
      from the two bright stars of my nipples.   I'm not
the phoenix in the classic narration of you, rising

                from the broken glass and the sun that travels
           through it to light this field on fire. I'm the glass—
              I have always wanted   to be taken

by you, to be made into a lake and reflected,
      wildly. Is it true what they say, that the best lovers
are always already inside of you,   a horizon

                so known it hurts? Haven't I always felt you
           bucking in my bones,   like history,   like land?
              You are a moth as old as my grandfather's

village and the waters he crossed to return
      to it, a winged body that believes in me
as a spark believes it will turn   to fire, as a fire

                believes, with its mouth open, that the black
           sky will continue   flooding   into it.

Many poems in this manuscript are indebted to Michèle Métail's scholarship on the 回文詩 or "reversible poem" tradition in Chinese poetry, especially her essays on the topic in *Wild Geese Returning,* translated by Jody Gladding. The following poems respond to specific reversible forms and poems that appear in her book:

> "窟" is written after Yuwen Xuzhong's "Autumn 3."

> "She's the only one who hears me sing" and "I could make my way through the grass" mimic a Chinese reversible form from the 5th century, 反覆 ("to turn and return"), where characters, in Métail's words, "are arranged in a circle, and the reader can begin with any character and read in one direction or the other."

> "何處別魂銷？" takes its title from a line in the reversible poem 《秋思》 ("Autumn Thoughts") by the Ming Dynasty poet Qiu Jun, which Métail and Gladding translate as "To what place do souls separated from bodies disappear?" The line in reverse, "銷魂別處何？" translates as "The place where vanished souls have gone, where is it?"

The following poems take titles from *Petrarch's Lyric Poems: The Rime Sparse and Other Lyrics,* translated by Robert M. Durling:

> "From what are you separated?" takes its title from *Rime Sparse 129.*

> "Your longed-for true form" takes its title from *Rime Sparse 16.*

> "I curse the day..." takes its epigraph from *Rime Sparse 22.*

> "From weeping into weeping" takes its title from *Rime Sparse 36.*

"My Grandfather Returns to 兗州 After the War" includes and adapts photo album captions written by my late paternal grandfather.

"Hitting the Ground" is written after "Strapping It On" by Sasha Warner-Berry.

"The Tear is Always Anything but Itself" takes its title and italicized line from the introduction to Eugenie Brinkema's *The Forms of the Affects.*

The phrase "happiest objects" in "My Sadness Was Not Like a Season" is attributed to Sara Ahmed.

The title "Clearly all about me winter reigns" or "四面又明明是嚴冬" is from Lu Xun's essay, 《風箏》("The Kite").

Acknowledgments

Thank you to the editors of the following journals and anthologies for publishing or reprinting versions of these poems: *The Adroit Journal, American Poetry Review, The Best American Poetry 2021, Best New Poets 2019, FENCE, Grist Journal, The Literary Review, The Margins, New Ohio Review, The Offing, Poetry Daily, Poetry Society of America's "In Their Own Words," The Pushcart Prize XLVI, Washington Square Review,* and *wildness.* This book was guided by the support of the communities at Asian American Writers' Workshop, Art Farm, Bread Loaf Writers' Conference, the Community of Writers, Fine Arts Work Center, Jentel, Lighthouse Works, Millay Arts, Monson Arts, and Storyknife.

Selected poems from this book appear in *I Watch the Boughs,* which won a 2020 Poetry Society of America Chapbook Fellowship. Gratitude to Gabrielle Calvocoressi and Brett Fletcher Lauer for making this possible.

Thank you to the entire Nightboat team for the deep attention and care in bringing 回 to publication: my editors, Gia Gonzales and Santiago Valencia, Lindsey Boldt, Jaye Elizabeth Elijah, Trisha Low, Stephen Motika, Rissa Hochberger, Caelan Nardone, Lina Bergamini, and Claire Zhang. To my blurbers, Anthony Cody, Cathy Park Hong, Sawako Nakayasu, and Brenda Shaughnessy—I am so lucky to carry your words with me.

Thank you to every writer who has been a friend to me and my poems. To Megan Pinto and Ariel Yelen, for carrying me through multiple drafts of this manuscript, for your true and joyous friendship. To Wendy Xu for helping me believe in these poems again. To the 2020 Margins Fellows; the 2019 Bread Loaf Waiters; to Angie Sijun Lou, Carolyn Orosz, Jack Schiff, and Sreshtha Sen. To my students, for their daring. To the entire Rutgers–Newark MFA family: I still can't believe my luck that we were brought together. Love to Ricardo Hernandez and Nhu Xuân Nguyễn, for all we've shared in line edits and life, and to Emily Caris, Ali Castleman, Sydney Jin Choi, Tracy Fuad, Andy Gallagher, Melissa Hartland, Ananda Lima, Simeon Marsalis, Maia Morgan, Lark Omura, Lauren Parrott, Grey Vild, Spencer Williams, and Ryan Lee Wong.

I am deeply indebted to my teachers. Thank you, Nancy Arena, Robert Cohen, Alice Elliott Dark, Vievee Francis, Rigoberto González, and especially to my advisors, Karin Gottshall, Cathy Park Hong, and Brenda Shaughnessy, for staying with me, poem by poem. A special thank you to Rachel Hadas for cutting out a review for *Wild Geese Returning* and bringing it to class for me one day, Marion Wells for her incredible scholarship on Petrarch, and Benjamin Graves for introducing me to the work of David L. Eng and Shinhee Han. To my teachers in the Middlebury Chinese department, who brought me back to my language: 感謝你們。

For accompanying me, thank you Doug, Kate, Sally, Drew, Delmeshia, and the Taiwanese kids™ in Massachusetts who raised me.

Thank you, Zain, for always protecting space for creation.

回 is dedicated to my entire family, through portals and across waters, whose histories and languages I am lucky to be bound to. Amber—thank you for reveling in the strange delights of life with me. To my mother, whose oceanic calligraphy appears on the cover of and throughout this book, for raising me in a world rich with colors, textures, and shapes. And to my father, the narrator of generations of stories—I write in the wake of your words.

EMILY LEE LUAN is the author of *I Watch the Boughs* (2021), selected by Gabrielle Calvocoressi for a Poetry Society of America Chapbook Fellowship. A former Margins Fellow at the Asian American Writers' Workshop and the recipient of a Pushcart Prize, her work has appeared in *The Best American Poetry 2021, Best New Poets 2019, American Poetry Review,* and elsewhere. She holds an MFA from Rutgers University–Newark.

NIGHTBOAT BOOKS

Nightboat Books, a nonprofit organization, seeks to develop audiences for writers whose work resists convention and transcends boundaries. We publish books rich with poignancy, intelligence, and risk. Please visit nightboat.org to learn about our titles and how you can support our future publications.

The following individuals have supported the publication of this book. We thank them for their generosity and commitment to the mission of Nightboat Books:

Anonymous (4)
Kazim Ali
Aviva Avnisan
Jean C. Ballantyne
The Robert C. Brooks Revocable Trust
Amanda Greenberger
Rachel Lithgow
Anne Marie Macari
Elizabeth Madans
Elizabeth Motika
Thomas Shardlow
Benjamin Taylor
Jerrie Whitfield & Richard Motika

This book is made possible, in part, by grants from the New York City Department of Cultural Affairs in partnership with the City Council and the New York State Council on the Arts Literature Program.